Investing For Beginners

Beginner's Ultimate Guide To Investing

Table of Contents

Introduction 3

Chapter 1: Financial Planning Tips............................. 6

Chapter 2: Saving and Investing 14

Chapter 3: Risk and Diversification........................... 22

Chapter 4: Asset Allocation 27

Chapter 5: Individual Stocks 33

Chapter 6: Mutual Funds and Index Funds 40

Chapter 7: Passive Investing vs. Active Investing....... 44

Chapter 8: Precious Metals – Gold, Platinum, Palladium and Silver 50

Chapter 9: Choosing A Brokerage Firm 54

Chapter 10: Real Estate Investing.............................. 60

Chapter 11: Starting And Running A Small Business ..63

Chapter 12: Tips For Success 69

Chapter 13: Mistakes To Avoid.................................. 74

Chapter 14: Keep Up With Your Progress 77

Chapter 15: Keep Up With The News........................ 80

Conclusion 83

Introduction

To enhance your financial performance, you need to have more than one income stream. One of the means to accomplish this is by maximizing different types of investments. It may be frustrating to get started due to the significant amount of choices that the marketplace has. However, you ought to be courageous and take the initial step required. Investing for novices is not that hard when you discover the basics.

Physical Guidance:

It is necessary to get somebody who will certainly guide you through the process to lessen chances of you making problems. The greatest individual to do this ought to be somebody who is skilled and has been in the industry for quite a while. You can easily decide to pay a person to suggest you. You can easily additionally find an individual that is willing to mentor you for a period.

Discover the lingo utilized in the industry:

If you are a major capitalist, you should know the various terms utilized so that you can easily communicate successfully with the pertinent stakeholders. You can brush up your investment nonsense utilizing some sources. You can check out investment books or use websites that cope with financial investments.

Create an economic plan:

This will certainly prevent you from making hasty decisions which will cost you in the long run. Stick to your plan at all times. It may be tempting to desert your plan for just what you think is a once in a lifetime deal. If the promotion appears too good to be true, it most likely is. Identify what kind of investments you need to make, way ahead of time depending on exactly how much danger you can afford to take.

Only invest funds that you can afford to lose:

This will certainly provide you a great deal of freedom to study on various possibilities. If you cannot afford to suffer from a loss, you will frequently be fretted about the economic complications you could get into in case you lose the money. This can cause you to make impulsive decisions. You should be ready to lose money in case an offer goes awry, but this should not be the objective.

Know what you're getting into:

Plainly know just how much net returns you will get from the investment. This is since in some cases you might make quite a profit then wind up spending the return paying your economic specialist their commission or charges. Discuss in advance what you will pay them and precisely how much money they should get.

Keep an eye on your financial investments:

This will help you understand the ideal actions to take being dependent on just what is going on in the market. You must be adequate enough to take the required steps if market trends change. To make your work easier, you can maximize various computer applications that will help you.

Core Basics:

Investing for beginners is not that challenging when you know the essentials of the business and exactly what to keep an eye on. Take your time as you stand a possibility of getting, even more, returns from long-term investments rather than short-term investments. Beware just how you manage your funds and just take well worked out dangers. Be relentless and do not give up.

Thanks again for downloading this book, I hope you enjoy it!

Chapter 1: Financial Planning Tips

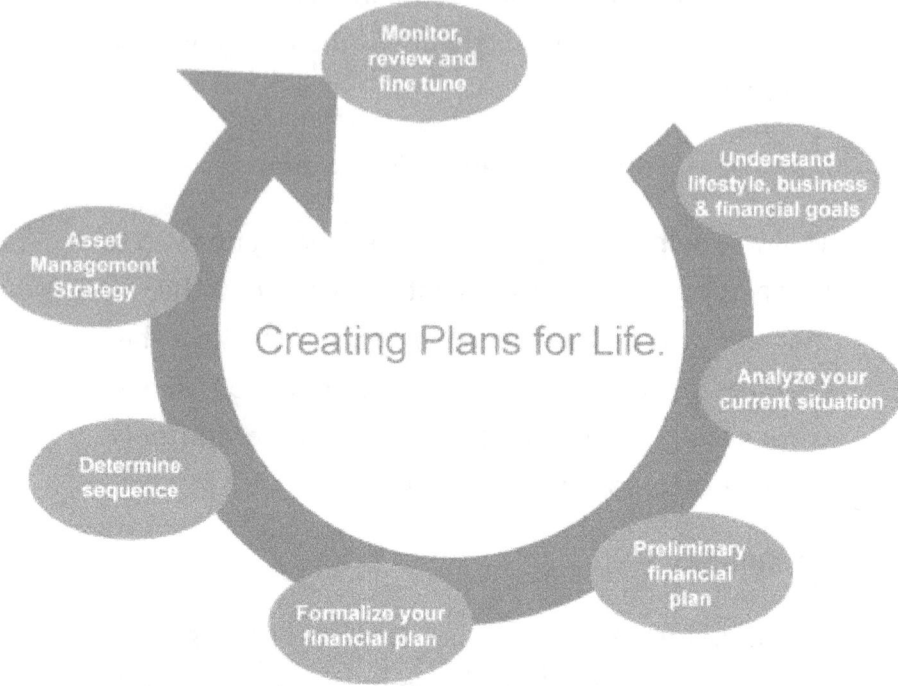

Are you wise about your finances? Have you done the proper planning to meet your future financial needs, like your children's college funds or your retirement? Sure, no one can tell the future, but it wouldn't hurt for you to be prepared financially for it. Plan today and worry less about the future. If you haven't even thought of financial planning before, it's time for you to start your personal project on financial planning, and this article will give you the basics to get started.

First of all, before embarking on anything in life we have to learn the basics, and in the case of financial planning, learning the basics means arming yourself with a financial education. You can do this by reading magazines, newspapers, books, and blogs - anything finance related. Keep yourself up to date on what's happening in the economy and how it translates to your personal finances.

Even if you have your personal financial planner, being more knowledgeable about investments, insurance, and other financial issues will ensure that you get the best financial plan out of your personal financial planner, because then you'll be able to discuss what works for you and what doesn't, without you having just to go along with your personal financial planner's advice because you have absolutely no idea what he's on about. Being more knowledgeable also allows you to smell a rat if your financial adviser is unethical, so you're more likely to spot bad advice when you hear one.

The next thing you should keep in mind before you embark on your personal financial planning project is that fear is bad. The recent trouble with the economy has filled investors with a sense of dread and fear, causing them to drop stocks from their investment portfolios and load up on safer, more conservative forms of investments, such as certificates of deposit and bonds. Some have even pulled the plug on their investments completely and decided not to take any risk. This in turn causes another problem because then they would not be able to meet their long-term financial goals, as their investment portfolios would be too conservative for them to earn any significant returns that they might need to retire in comfort. Worse still if they choose to stop saving, on top of ceasing their investments. Therefore it is important for you not simply to react to the market fluctuations and follow the masses blindly.

Equip yourself with adequate knowledge to study the trends of the various financial instruments and decide wisely.

If you aren't already investing, you should consider starting right now. Sure, a lot of people don't like to think about investing because investing can be scary, especially with the economic outlook these days. The word "investing" also comes with the preconceived notion that only the rich and affluent can afford to do, or it requires one to be a skilled professional before they can invest. That couldn't be further from the truth; anyone can invest, and rightfully should. Most people think the only way to earn extra income is to work, work, and work. Overtime. What they don't realize is that investing gives them the opportunity to let their money work for them; they get to save on time but still get to earn some money on their downtime.

If you are already considering on investing but aren't sure of your finances, then it's time to get your finances organized. Your money is in a constant cycle; there's inflow and there's outflow. What you want to do is to ensure that your inflow is significantly larger than your outflow at the end of the day. Example, make more than you spend basically. If you've got a ton of bills to pay and multiple bank accounts to keep track of, keeping track of your finances can be a real headache.

Organizing your finances can save you a lot of time, so you should consider using a personal finance plan software. Take a few minutes to key in your cash inflows and outflows will help you stay on top of your finances. This software doesn't even need to be anything sophisticated like an accountant would use but even the good old Microsoft Excel would work.

There are many processes involved in a comprehensive financial planning. The above points are just a few suggestions for you to get started on your personal project on financial planning so that you'll be well on your way to a financially secured future....

Financial planning requires establishing goals and developing a strategic plan which can expedite the process. Whether you're buying a house, starting a business, saving for higher education, working towards retirement, investing in real estate, yeah you get it... Basically anything you want in life. Financial planning is the key to achieving success.

Financial planning has always been important, but in today's economy, it is more important than ever. Regrettably, a large majority of Americans are struggling just to provide the basics, let alone save money for the future. However, with knowledge and willpower, most people can find a way to save a few extra bucks. It simply requires review of current finances to determine where expenses can be reduced or income increased such eating out instead of staying in.

The first step in developing a financial plan requires individuals to review their income and expenses. Many people do not realize how much money they spend on unnecessary items. One simple strategy to determine where your money goes is to track every penny spent over the course of one month. Write down the amount spent and what was purchased.

Then review to determine where expenses can be reduced.

If you spend $20 per week on morning coffee or fast food lunches, consider buying a travel mug and brown bag lunches instead. Deposit the saved funds into a high-interest savings account. Over the long haul, saving $10 per week can eventually turn into thousands of dollars while earning interest.

Financial guru, Suze Orman, suggests saving a minimum of 10-percent of income. She recommends perceiving savings deposits as a regular bill and encourages consumers to get in the habit of paying their self as well as their creditors.

Dave Ramsey is another financial wizard that provides exceptional financial planning tools via his website. Ramsey offers a no-nonsense approach to debt management while providing an arsenal of financial planning information. Visitors can learn how to obtain financial freedom regardless of their monthly earnings.

Individuals with multiple debts might benefit from credit counseling. Individuals with low incomes may qualify for low-cost counseling through non-profit agencies which use sliding scales to determine fees. Depending on the amount of earned income some people are eligible for no-cost counseling. The National Foundation for Credit Counseling offers a list of nationwide credit counselors via their website at NFCC.org.

The Internet is also a good source for obtaining information about financial planning options. Much of the information is offered at no cost. Before investing money into financial planning workshops, it is important to engage in due diligence and determine the credibility of the person or company offering the information. Always conduct research online or check with the Better Business Bureau to determine if any complaints have been filed.

Many people find working with a certified financial planner is a way to build a solid financial plan. These professionals are trained to help individuals and couples achieve short and long-term investment goals through review of income, expenses and implementation of investment strategies.

Consumers can find a list of certified financial planners, along with financial planning tools, resources, and online webinars through the Financial Planning Association website at FPAforFinancialPlanning.org. Visitors can peruse informative articles regarding saving for college, buying a house, estate planning, retirement planning, and much more.

The sooner financial planning strategies are implemented, the sooner wealth can be built. However, it is important to conduct research to determine which strategies are best suited for your personal investment goals. Afterward, develop an investment and savings plan, make a commitment, and stick to it!

Chapter 2: Saving and Investing

The future is extremely unpredictable, and it is difficult to ascertain the kind of situations that we would have to face in the coming days and years. That is why it is extremely important and vital to invest and save money in a strategic and proper manner.

Some of the reasons why saving money are important are as follows-

Emergency Funds:

To tackle emergencies in a proper manner, you need to have a substantial amount of money that you have saved over a period. These emergencies could include any number of things like building a new roof, unexpected medical expenses, sudden layoff leading to loss of steady income, etc.

Improvement in life expectancy:

As medicines and public health facilities improve, the average life expectancy of an individual is all set to rise. This means that you would require more money to maintain the same quality and standard of life over the years.

The volatility of social security:

Even if the government in your country provides social security, it cannot be considered as the main source of income. Social security, at best, can be a small part of your additional income and in no way should you depend on it entirely for your daily expenses. If at any time, social security plans are withdrawn, you will be left with no source of income and that can become a major hurdle in your financial independence.

Education and other expenses:

The cost of both private and public education is increasing every single year. Not just that, many daily needs are also becoming more expensive. So to live a comfortable life, it is of utmost necessity that you save money at every stage possible.

Investment plans are one of the best ways that can help you save money in an easy and simple manner. Furthermore, it becomes much easier to manage your investments when individuals are in the habit to save on a regular basis. It is, therefore, important to balance both your personal income and expenditure on a monthly basis before you can invest your money in a proper manner.

Some steps that you can follow to save money in a better manner, include-

Create a budget to track your expenses on a monthly basis:

Creating a budget will help you identify your spending areas and in turn, regulate cash flow. When you track your expense against your budget in a proper manner, it will also help you save money by ensuring that you do not spend money on things that you do not need.

Ensure that you pay off your current credit card debts:

Paying off your credit card debt will help you save money in the long run. Credit card companies charge a huge interest along with principal investments. When you pay off your credit card debts in time, you ensure that you save money that you would otherwise have spent on paying off the interests.

Save some part of your salary every month for emergencies:

Emergencies often come unannounced. When you save money every month for unexpected emergencies, it ensures that it does not create a huge dent in your financial resources. A good idea to save these funds is through a savings account or a money-market mutual fund.

Invest in education, pension, and insurance retirement plans:

Investing in insurance plans ensures that you get life cover, education cover and retirement cover. Not only do you get tax exceptions, but you also ensure good return when you require money the most.

Invest in a diversified investment program or systematic investment plan:

If you do not mind taking risks, investing in the equity-based mutual fund is a good idea. Otherwise, you can invest in bonds and other safe securities. Keep in mind of your own objectives before you decide to invest in a particular investment plan.

Invest in life insurance policies:

Life insurance policies are one of the best ways to invest your money so that you are not just prepared for any eventuality but can earn rich returns as well. A good life investment policy will not just secure your future but will also help you provide for the financial independence and security of your loved ones.

Hence, when your saving plans are in place, it will ensure that your investments are protected and safeguarded at all times. At all times, make sure that your extra money is invested in good investment plans so that you can reap rich dividends in the future. Good saving plans and investment plans are extremely important in this volatile and ever-changing economic environment. In the end, saving and investing money is very important and will help you live a more comfortable life in the long run.

Life has many milestones to be achieved like having your family car, child's education and marriage, retirement planning, etc. Slowly and steadily each milestone has to be handled with care and with proper finance backup so that you live with pride and happiness in the society. However, this is all possible if you have a regular savings approach to achieve all this.

While everyone aims to set upon their long or short term goals, it is important to sit with your financial manager and discuss the options open to you so that you have a systematic and streamlined plan to reap the benefits time-to-time as per the requirement of your goals.

While the market is flooded with various investment option such as gold, mutual funds, stocks, etc. Life insurance is one of the best saving plans which needs to be given a thought upon. These plans are built with an aim to stay away from all the worries of the future when there is a solid long-term savings and protection plan for people.

The article discusses few tips while strategizing for yourself amongst the best saving plans available in insurance segment-

Savings Discipline:

By putting aside a part of your savings into life insurance savings plan you will not only build the habit of disciplined saving but will also shelter your family with an insurance cover. It additionally helps you grow and develop an adequate amount of wealth through market linked investments. Putting little savings every month in these plans will help you accumulate funds which your family can benefit from in future.

Enjoy Short term goals:

Investing money in saving plans on a regular basis help money grow in the compound method. Therefore, the earning can be utilized to fulfill short-term goals as well as years from now what you have accumulated can let you fulfill bigger goals in life.

Inflation control:

When you keep enough income to counter monthly expenses and contribute the rest to a long term savings plan, this will help you grow your money well. When the money grows it will be capable enough to counter the inflation costs in future. Thus your worries about the future seem to be so much more under control

Emergency fund:

Once you start investing in one of the best saving plans of your choice, you have the ability to settle down your loans or any other emergency requirements with the accumulating benefits over the years. If you need help in emergencies, the policy earnings are always a helping hand for you.

Switch Funds:

The good part of the saving plan is that it allows you to switch funds and change the proportion in which the premium is invested. At any moment if your financial expert's recommendation funds are not working for you, then you can take a call and switch it as per your convenience at no extra costs for certain switching. Switching involves changing the proportion by investing more in certain funds and fewer others. It gives the flexibility to change the proportion of savings depending on your risk appetite and the market environment from time to time.

Best saving plans are like an art which can be sketched with your hard work, determination and affordability. It is important to buy a policy considering your income, monthly expenses, spending habits and standard of living. Always draft a plan that you can afford that offers enough financial assistance and at the same time you don't have to compromise on regular spending habits. Long term saving plans are the best companion during the thick and thin times in life.

Chapter 3: Risk and Diversification

Current increases in the volatility of the financial markets have many investors thinking about their portfolios and wondering if they should make changes. This is, therefore, an excellent time to discuss the importance of maintaining a disciplined approach to diversified investing.

Here are four key points to keep in mind about disciplined and diversified investing during periods of market volatility:

1) Diversification is a method designed to reduce risk.

In the financial markets, risk and reward go together. Higher reward investments tend to carry greater risk. Although all investors would like nothing better than a high reward investment that carries low risk, it is important to remember how rare that is. When one diversifies one's portfolio, it is to reduce risk. We do not diversify to maximize reward; rather we diversify to reduce risk and portfolio volatility.

2) If one's portfolio is properly diversified, then one need not carry around a great deal of anxiety about the daily ups and downs of the market. With reduced volatility that proper diversification brings, one need not become either exultant in an upmarket or dejected in a downward market. Instead one

maintains a centered approach to long-term investing - not overreacting to market volatility.

3) Asset allocation and diversification are best done by calendar rather than by reactivity to market conditions. One of the biggest traps for investors is to get excited and buy when markets are rising (thereby buying high) and to get scared and sell when markets are falling (thereby selling low). The best way to avoid this is to review one's asset allocation at a regularly scheduled account review.

4) One of the best ways to build wealth is to take a longer time horizon to your investments. Sound investments held over a long time horizon is the approach that we find works best. As Warren Buffet has said, "in the short term, the stock market is a voting machine, in the long-term, it is a weighing machine." In a short time horizon, emotions and group psychology rule the ups and downs of the markets. In the long term, the fundamental value of sound investments will rule the day.

Investors may well be in a better position to ride out the short-term volatility we see in today's markets by maintaining the discipline of diversified asset allocation with a longer time horizon.

Financial diversification simply lets you apply the age-old adage of "not putting all your eggs in one basket." In practical terms, it means that you take your savings and spread your savings among different type of investment options. This type of investment does take some work, and it will take some planning on your part.

This leaves the question of why. Why would anyone put forth the time and energy to diversify their portfolio? The answer comes down to risk. Financial diversification is designed to help minimize overall risk to gain long-term, steady returns.

If all your eggs are in one basket and the basket happens to get run over a car, you may be left with nothing. Similarly, if you were one of the ones who invested their entire future of savings in Enron, you may be working a second or third job to pay your bills in retirement.

If you want to minimize your financial risk, it is time to diversify. Some tips to help you achieve this goal-

Split your portfolio up among 3 or 4 different industries:

Do not put all of your savings into real estate or oil or the newest "gadget" your neighbor created. Making this type of split helps you to weather the downturns in one industry without seeing your savings substantially drop.

Choose different types of investments:

Some types include stocks, bonds and cash. You can put money into a savings account, which is very stable because of FDIC insurance, but has a lower interest rate. The stability of bonds and stocks depend on upon the type of stock or bond you wish to purchase. It is important to research your specific investment to make sure you know all the pros and cons of your choice.

Do not limit to one only:

If you choose to invest in stocks and bonds, make sure you purchase more than just one stock or bond. That way, if the one company in which you own stock declares bankruptcy, you are not hit as hard as you would be if you owned stock in multiple companies. If you are unsure of how to select stocks, then check out mutual funds.

Financial diversification can take some time for research and some effort to understand your options. Although many people handle their investment choices and manage their portfolios, others choose to find a financial manager to do that for them.

No matter the amount you have in your egg basket, financial diversification provides a safer path to a more comfortable future without the worries of a single kick making you homeless.

Chapter 4: Asset Allocation

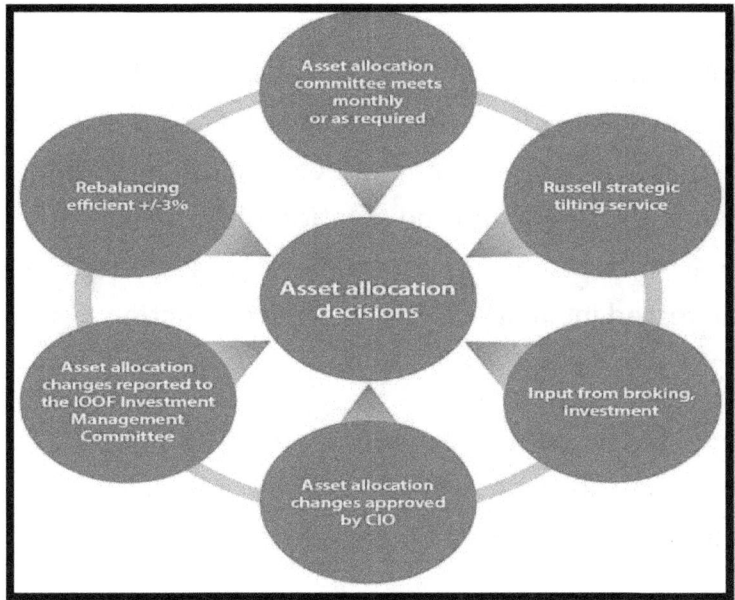

Everyone wants to have more money. Moreover, people want to achieve that state of financial freedom that describes a level of success that could be described as "financial independence." Some say that the wealthiest 5% of individuals have more than the 95% put together between them regarding financial net worth. These 5% also control 95% of the money whether it'd be business, tax or personal money.

Why do people desire money success? There are too many reasons to list here. Perhaps you could make a list yourself. Writing 100 reasons why to decide to be wealthy is a valuable exercise taught in many financial success seminars.

Allocation of assets can be considered a key to financial success. But what exactly is asset allocation? And what are its cause and effect relationship in the building of wealth and the creation of financial success? There are a large number of assets that can be invested in. Firstly let's make the distinction between asset and liability.

Simply put, an asset is something that probably cost you money and either makes money or increases in value. Something like a house is an example of this.

A liability is something that costs money and decreases in value. A car is a good example of a liability. Although a motor vehicle is an "asset" in that it has its benefits, in terms of financial key to asset allocation, a car decreases in value and keeps costing you money at the same time (usually, unless it is a classic car for example - but then you wouldn't want to drive it too much to keep the mileage low). Similarly "toys" such as electronic goods are usually liabilities.

A house can be an asset, because after you buy it after you have made renovations or improvements along with the historical evidence of supply and demand action in the market, the value can go up. The same is true of a successful business. You channel money into a business first and after establishing the business, it can pay for many years to come.

Allocation of liquid assets is what we are considering here. With many investment opportunities available to the person with virtually any amount of capital, it is a challenge to find the right opportunity and to allocate financial assets correctly for their continued growth and your increasing wealth.

Here are a few-

A portfolio of stocks is one possibility:

For the person with a higher risk appetite, some skill, training in creating a portfolio, managing losses and finding the best stocks. This way has made many Americans very wealthy.

Nowadays there are also managed mutual funds (investment funds) whose managers are professionals at asset allocation in the stock market. This is lower risk than individual stock investing, but still carries a risk. Some funds have very good returns, but it is worth always looking at the performance in the long term (i.e. 5-10 years) and many other factors, such as manager's historical performance, sector, and country, etc. "Always consult your financial advisor before taking a decision" is the forewarning when mentioning anything like this, and applies here too. Trading the foreign exchange market is a possibility also (forex) again with high risk associated and industry warnings attached.

The advantage of funds over a stock portfolio is that you get automatic diversification within the portfolio but without having to do the research on each of the companies yourself. Instead, you are delegating a professional money manager to do that for you. Online information is quite good and often free if you look in the right places for fund performance histories, portfolios, and management.

A lower risk alternative to stock markets is the market in government bonds. Over the long term, bonds do not compare so highly to equities markets as regards to returns. A bond will pay a fixed return over time (long term).

Diversification is key:

Starting a business, investing in equities capital markets, real estate and long-term safer investments will create balance in your portfolio and help you to achieve financial independence with less stress and worry. The chances are that if you spread your investment, there will be more likelihood in the event of one investment heading south, another will either hedge or outperform the unsuccessful in overall profitability.

Research professional advice from someone who is practicing what they are preaching as well as keeping a close management eye on your portfolio will help identify strengths and weaknesses in the portfolio and allow the investor to change, sell or increase investment where and when appropriate to do so.

Asset allocation is one of the ways on how to manage risks. In asset allocation, your money will be allocated to different investments so that there is lower risk involved. Before investing or choosing your vehicles, these questions must first be answered:

1. Where will I use the money (is it to purchase a dream car, a house or to pay for next year's vacation)?
2. How much risk can I tolerate?

The question of for what purpose will the money be used will determine the length of time the investment will run. It is because the longer the time, the higher probability for it to have a large capital gain. That is the rule in investing. We can often hear financial advisors ask us this same question because the first rule of investing is that first, you should have a plan.

There are many types of investments out there and knowing the right one for you will make the whole experience educational and agreeable.

The second question will determine how much risk an investor is willing to take. In this way, you and your financial advisor can clearly map out the possibilities available for you should you decide to start with a low-risk investment. It is also advisable to know that low-key or low-risk investments have the possibility to offer you with lesser capital gains. You have to keep that in mind because it is utterly a shame to be investing in low key investments and wonder why you're getting very little percentage rate increase.

There are three types of assets investments. These are cash, stocks and bonds. You may play with these three types to have a more diverse investment portfolio. You may allocate your money through these three types of investments. There is an advantage through this so that you can easily offset it once one starts to show signs of declining.

Asset Allocation activity is a wise choice and a great equalizer for your investment. It is also a best and classic example of managing risks.

Chapter 5: Individual Stocks

Most people do not realize that a lot of stocks and shares belong to individual investors. Consequently, individual investors contribute more than three billion dollars in the stock market and bonds. Individuals rely on professional advisors for suggestions once the stocks and bonds are purchased.

There are various options for investing in the stock market. One option for an individual is mutual funds which allow companies to select where to invest the money in the stock market. Also, brokerage funds can be used to trade stocks.

Investment in stocks is a good strategy for ensuring your long-term financial stability. To maximize your earnings from investing in stocks you have to get your stock investing basics right. This article discusses some tips that you can use for understanding the basics of stock investing.

For stock investing basics we should focus on two criteria:

1. Examine the absolute gross profit attained for each share. Gross profit may be taken as a percentage that compares the middle selling price of stock with the middle buying price of that stock. Brokerage fees, government levies

and all other additional costs should not be included in the absolute gross profit calculations.
2. Also, the individual should enquire about the changes of the share market index which is based on the major shares in the stock market.

Understanding the basics of investing leads to choosing successful stocks, but it is also important to remember that there is a potential downside to investing. It is important always to have some backup if the stocks are not successful.

There are sustained periods of downward movements for share prices. This phase of the market is known as the 'bear phase.' In a strong bear market, the good shares get dragged down with the others. This is a good time to buy such shares for the purpose of long-term investing.

It is difficult to make an accurate investment decision every time. Thus a loss minimisation plan is necessary for the protection of long term profits. Understanding and learning the basics that are discussed in this article will allow you to become a successful stock investor.

Most investors have no idea when to buy and sell stocks. There are many factors that can go into the decision-making process, and we are constantly bombarded by opinions from CNBC, the Wall Street Journal, Investor's Business Daily and a variety of other media outlets.

So how does the individual investor or trader determine when to buy and sell stocks? First of all, the individual must conduct an assessment of themselves to determine how even to approach answering this question. Here are some questions you should ask yourself...

1. How much time do you have to devote to analyze the stock market and individual stocks?
2. How much risk capital do you have?
3. What are your long-term and short-term financial goals?
4. How safe is your present job situation?
5. How much can you set aside and save each month for your investments?
6. What is your tolerance for risk?
7. What do you know about what drives stock prices?
8. How much time do you have to monitor your investments/trades?

These are just a few questions you need to ask yourself BEFORE you get started in trying to trade stocks profitably. In reality, however, trading stocks is not rocket science, but you need to get a handle on your personal situation to determine how you can develop a strategy suitable to your needs and desires.

For instance, if you don't have the ability to monitor your trades throughout the day, then you have no business operating as a short-term trader, or day trader. Also, if you don't have enough money saved to cover your expenses for at least a few months, then you should not be relying on your trading/investments to provide income for yourself.

Once you have assessed your situation and goals, it is time to educate yourself about the market. What exactly causes the price of stock to move up or down? The very basic cause is supply and demand. You should realize that there are a finite number of shares available for any given company. The issuing common stock is one way a company raises money for its capital needs. If the demand for a stock outweighs the supply of the stock, the price will rise. If the supply exceeds demand, the price will fall.

Factors that drive the demand for a stock include its earnings, its return on equity, its dividend, or maybe it is producing a hot new product that will be valuable to consumers. This is what the analysts on CNBC are trying to do...determine the demand for a stock.

Most people should not even try to speculate about future demand for a stock. The price of the stock itself will tell you whether the company is currently in favor with investors, or out of favor. At any given time, there are always companies whose shares are rising in price, so it makes no sense for the individual investor to buy stock in a company when the price of that stock is falling.

The fact of the matter is, the analysts hired by the big Wall Street companies do not have any better idea about whether a company's stock price will go up or down than the individual investor unless they obtain some information illegally which is called insider trading. With that in mind, the best course of action for individual investors is to ignore the analysts and do their homework.

So, back to the original question...when to buy and sell stocks:

The individual needs to develop a plan and strategy for trading and to invest in stocks. Since most people do not have the capital to wait out an investment that is falling in price, the first good idea is to focus on stocks that have been rising in price. If an investor wants to see profits fairly quickly, they should only focus on stocks that are rising in price. This fact alone tells the investor that there is underlying demand for that stock.

Next, the trader should determine how they can enter a position and keep their risk at a minimum. With that in mind, it is a good idea to wait for a stock that is rising in price to undergo a period where that price consolidates. By this, we mean that the price stops rising, and essentially moves sideways, or up and down within a narrow price range. This allows the opportunity to define risk by identifying a point where buying the stock allows for instant profitability while at the same time identifying a price point where the trader will exit the position if for some reason the stock begins falling in price. What the trader wants to do is hop on board the stock when it regains its momentum to the upside, but at the same time limits his/her risk in the position.

There are many strategies that can achieve this goal, and it is beyond the scope of this article to identify even just a few of them. However, the trader or individual investor would be wise to do some research on the idea of trend following as it applies to the financial markets. Big money in the markets is made by capturing trends, and the traders who do this best, tend to be the most successful. If you can develop a strategy that will allow you to ride a stock for most of its uptrend, then you will have a great opportunity for long-term profitability.

Successful investing or trading is quite simple. You must buy stocks when they are rising in price and sell stocks when they are falling in price. Unfortunately, this is counterintuitive, because most people want to buy things when they are cheap. However, if you view a stock as you would any quality product, then you will soon realize that you must pay for quality. A stock that is cheap is cheap for a reason…because it is not a good product. Therefore, if you simply focus on stocks that are rising in price, you will have a leg up on most other investors.

Chapter 6: Mutual Funds and Index Funds

There are dozens of publications in bookshops and newspaper advertising mentioning all the best mutual funds for this year! All claiming to know what are the best mutual fund.

Investing bag seems simple, but it is not. It requires a bit of sacrifice and dedication to understanding how it works.

The investment stock market mutual funds recommendation could be summarized in four simple words: "Buy an index fund." Yes, this option of investing may sound simple but do you understand what a background that is indexing? A mutual fund is simply a collection of actions and bonds. Most mutual funds are an administrator, "which means that you as a fund investor are paying an annual fee for that person to invest in the stock market and the stock market and buy and sell shares for you.

Although you would think that mutual funds provide benefits to shareholders employing "experts "to choose the actions, the sad truth is that most of these funds have a poor performance. If you have your 401K and has its money in mutual funds only then think over the next ten years is going to lose money, or not going to have if you spent the few hours a month on managing their money.

The easiest way for the funds is:

Confuse the enemy and will have at your side. I state this because I understand a background report or the monthly statement is more complicated than taking a Ph.D. in Biotechnology. Never tell when it is their contribution and when operating costs and performance of the specified month. Additionally, the cost of management is the acquisition cost of shares.

When generally investing in the stock market through mutual funds has returned an average of 2% below the average of the stock indices. The average value of the bag is about 11 % per year. Additionally, we have to deduct administrative costs and special charges and the bottom end could be talking about a 4% or 5%, almost the same as leaving your money in a CD or fixed-term deposit. Investing in a fund puts you in the passenger seat of a bus that you may not serve the destination, and you have no control.

Advantages of investing in mutual funds-

Diversification:

Buying a mutual fund provides take immediate participation in a group of companies without having to spend in commissions for the purchase of each action individually. You can spread the risk in different sectors and sizes of companies according to the background model.

Liquidity:

As individual stocks, mutual fund investment can turn into instant cash.

Risk:

You can choose to invest in hedge funds, medium and low risk. This results in final performance.

Participation:

If your company offers Matching Funds, you could put a percentage of the 401K in it and you could double your savings over time.

Investing in the stock market directly can leave the best rewards, but how to choose the right actions?

A strategy easy to understand is this:

Let 50% of the money free in your 401K so you can move the rest into an IRA or IRA rollover or how much handling yourselves handled withdrawals. Choose from different backgrounds the best strategies and best companies. This will give you greater flexibility and may follow the advice of experts. Assess the actions that you have chosen to compare the fund's performance where he still has his 25%.

In the end, I assure you that you have made the best choice to diversify, reduce costs and increase profits from their investments.

Chapter 7: Passive Investing vs. Active Investing

While most people get excited about trading, it is the investor that will triumph in the long run. Anyone who looks for capital gain is classified as a trader. Investors, on the other hand, focus on building sustainable and longer term cash flow and passive income. An investor will eventually have an upper hand over traders because an investor acquires an asset for the long run and not for the short.

Capital Gain:

A trader will keep making new trades by buying and selling while a true investor will make one important commitment and ride it all the way. With each new trade, a trader assumes the new risk. An investor looks at the big picture and buys into appreciating assets. With time, the capital gain is almost certain without assuming the unnecessary risk and emotional stress.

Consistent Passive Income and Growing Income:

Because a trader focuses only in capital gain, they have to keep making new trades and taking on new risk. An investor waits for the right opportunity to get into the right investment that will continue to provide passive income for many years to come. Typically, an investor should get into positions that will provide an immediate 6% to 8% initial rate of return with the growth potential of 12% to 15% per year. Of course, without saying, the higher, the better. With an immediate passive income stream with a potential for future growth of income within the next two years, the life of an investor is financially secured and stress-free.

Income Continues to Grow In-Line With Inflation:

It is extremely important that your buying power increases with time. The only way to be sure is that your income growth is faster than the inflation rate. It is unwise to take the inflation rate provided by our governments as an indication as that is normally lower that the actual rate. A good measurement is against the rise in gasoline cost as it will affect all other products and services. A smart investor will structure his investments to grow fast that the unofficial inflation rate to protect his buying power and wealth. Not much can be said of a trade as a trader will only make more trades to survive. More trades with new risk exposure could mean more harm to a trader. Even more dangerous when there is some desperation to maintain the ever increasing expenses of current lifestyle.

Tax Rate:

Like it or not, the tax remains one of our highest expenses. For most of us, it is the highest expense that we have. There are all sorts of taxes when it comes to investing. One that is obvious for many of us in Malaysia when it comes to investing is Real Estate Gain Tax. A trader or flipper who buys and sells Real Estate will have to pay if their holding of the asset is less than five years. An investor who holds on to the property for more than five years does not need to worry about this. In some countries like America, there is also a capital gain tax on the stock appreciation. It makes much more sense to invest in something that you know will have good growth potential regarding cash flow and capital appreciation - ride the wave and sell off years later to avoid being taxed at all.

Cost of Doing Business:

A trader typically will focus on capital gain. Most traders do not mind paying as these are part of the business. But the bill runs up pretty fast, and these expenses eat into the overall profit. If a trader trades the stock market, the brokerage fees run up real fast as compared to an investor who buys and rarely sells. The brokerage fees over a year can have a significant impact on your overall return on investment. Likewise in Real Estate, legal fees, and stamp duties can take a significant percentage of a trader's profit. A Real Estate Investor who focus on cash flow and passive income only pays for the legal fees once and enjoy the benefit of the positive cash flow for years to come.

Exponential Growth Through Compounded Interest:

Before committing to an asset, a true investor would have already had a good idea of the growth rate for the next ten years - better still 20 years. With a targeted growth rate of only 12% per year, a patient but smart investor knows that it takes less than 6 years to double his net worth. Although I know some traders who can double their net worth in less time, I know that it requires plenty of skill, experience, and emotional discipline. Unfortunately, there are not many of such traders out there in the market.

A smart investor, with time, will continue to compound his wealth through the amazing power of compounded interest. Compounded Interest is has been described by Albert Einstein as "the most powerful force in the universe." Many large financial institutions have used compounded interest to their maximum advantage. A true investor will use this to grow his wealth exponentially. Unfortunately, for a trader, due to the nature of their market approach, this powerful tool is not made available.

Stress and Emotional State:

Just imagine this, a new trade equals to new risk and with no stable cash flow or passive income, every trade can be stressful. In the Real Estate where the value of each transaction is typically higher, the stress level increases. Trading requires plenty of energy and focus.

Some traders that I have met are glued to their notebook because every tick or price movement counts. This type of 'investment' surely is not suitable for the faint hearted especially when you know that your decision in that very moment will affect your retirement and the financial future of your family. An investor is calm because an investor is not affected by market movements or Real Estate development. An investor's primary focus is generating positive cash flow with very little effort.

Investing is a serious part of your life. It is not about excitement. It is not about generating fast money. Investments should be safe. Investment decisions should be made with little emotions. If you know how, and almost certainly with time, your investments goals can be fulfilled. With all the advantages that an investor has over a trader, would you like to be a trader or an investor? Perhaps look at your current investment strategies, is it for capital gain or is it for cash flow?

Your decision to be a trader or investor will affect your financial future significantly.

Chapter 8: Precious Metals – Gold, Platinum, Palladium and Silver

Over the years, the United States has minted many types of silver coins. The current silver dollar coin is the American Silver Eagle with． 999 silver bullion. But, when people speak of silver dollars in a coin collection they are typically referring to the coins made in the late 19th and early 20th centuries, the Morgan Silver Dollar. If we want to find out what is so special about this coin, we first need to step back in history.

The Morgan Silver Dollar was authorized by the Bland-Allison Act, February 28, 1878. Minting of the coin began in 1878 and ran till 1904. It was again minted from 1921 until 1935. Up until 1965, silver coins minted by the US were all silver. This is one reason why the Morgan Silver Dollar is in such demand among collectors.

The Morgan Silver Dollar takes its name from George T. Morgan, its designer. This particular coin has Lady Liberty on the front side (obverse) and an American eagle on the back side (reverse). Even people who are not coin collectors or investors in silver find this silver dollar very appealing to look at. The coin commemorates the expansion westward that the U. S. was undergoing at that point in history.

At the time that the Morgan Silver Dollar was minted, the silver rush was going on in the West. As such, the United States Mint cast more coins than were necessary for legal tender. Huge numbers of uncirculated coins were locked away until 1960. A good number of the coins were melted down and used for other coins. It is not difficult to find an uncirculated Morgan coin today.

A proof coin is minted especially for collectors and is never meant to be circulated. Proof coins are the rarest and extremely valuable. Graded Mint State 65 (MS-65) and the Gem Uncirculated coins are the second most sought after of this particular coin. Although the face value of the Morgan Silver Dollar is one dollar, the silver it contains is worth far more. Every Morgan dollar has. 77344 troy ounces (oz) of silver. This is equivalent to. 858575171318 avoirdupois ounces (oz), the commonly used measurement in the States. The PCGS and NGC have more credibility in the world of coin collecting and grading than do smaller organizations. As such, coins graded by PCGS and NGC have a higher value as compared with coins graded by smaller companies.

One of the reasons that silver is a more prudent and safe investment as compared to other precious metals such as gold, palladium or platinum is that coin collectors do not tend to sell their collections. This makes the market demand hold steady and is one reasons why the silver market has been a safe investment for four decades. Additionally, some people like to invest in silver coins to broaden their investment portfolio.

Silver is used in many more industrial applications than gold, platinum or palladium. The demand is so great for silver that the supply cannot keep up. In fact, the silver mining industry is running short of available above-ground silver to mine. This demand keeps the price of silver growing.

Coins, in general, are simple to store at home in a flood and fire safe vault or at the bank in a secure safe deposit box. The coins are also easy to transport. No large truck necessary. Simply put the coins in a box in your car and away you go.

Another definite advantage to investing in the Morgan silver coins is that most people can afford to start investing fairly easily. Except for the proof coins, this is not the coin of the elite collector. Additionally, if the financial world took another downturn, the coins are legal U. S. Currency and can be used as such immediately. Not needing to worry about finding a buyer to liquidize assets makes this coin even more attractive as an investment. Collecting silver coins as an investment is a wise and prudent financial move that will hold its value for years to come.

Chapter 9: Choosing A Brokerage Firm

An online brokerage firm allows consumers to exercise more control over their investing activities. An online brokerage firm gives investors a chance to pick and choose their funds and stocks without worrying about what time it is. Online portfolios can be monitored at any time throughout the day or night. This is great in providing that extra boost of security for many. Everyone knows that a happy customer is one that will continue using the services that a company has to offer. This means online options are promoting a wide range of fee choices, tools, services and as well as personal touches to entice potential investors.

There are many advantages to turning to online means to conduct your investing business. The first deals with not having to shell out high commission rates for a full-service broker. It is up to you to choose which investments to become a part of. To make sure you are getting the most out of the service, you should research all potential online firms. Sometimes there is more than one low commission fee per trade. Although there may be a higher fee for the commission, you may be able to enjoy access to a wide range of tools that allow you to conduct better research when paying a higher cost. Choosing a lower commission fee requires that you maintain higher minimum balances. You should always compare various balance requirements, as well as the fees to maintain your service.

Many online brokerage firms offer a sense of trustworthiness and professionalism that is especially gratifying for a first-time investor. There are many different aspects of the service to look out for, including financial glossaries, terms, news headlines and as well as phone customer support. Just remember that the customer service part of the online firm only helps with website issues and cannot give you any advice on your investments.

With Share builder, there are tons of selections to consider when looking for online banking services. There are a lot of various funds and stocks to choose from when you are ready to create a portfolio. Buying and selling through this service is also easier because you will be dealing with real-time actions. Share builder offers three different investment plans to look into. Recurring plans include a Basic option, as well as a Standard choice. For those that wish for more capabilities with their plan, there is a selection called Advantage. As for fees, the Basic plan has no monthly fee attached. A charge not surpassing $5 is associated with each investment. Limit orders are less than $20.

Another advantage to choosing this option is that there are no account or investment minimums that you have to worry about. There are also no inactivity fees.

As you sift through the many different online firms, you should conduct research on each and every potential selection. This allows you to make the best-informed decision. After all, this is your money we're talking about. Don't you want the best to handle your future funds?

Another option is to attach yourself and your money to Ameritrade services, which offers a commission fee that costs below $11 for stock market orders. This is the same fee charged for limit orders. Commissions regarding mutual funds are under $18 when buying or selling of various funds has taken place. You may also select to do business with margin accounts or short accounts.

You may opt to do business with Ameritrade, which requires a minimum balance of $1000. Accessing the individual account will only take less than $20 in fees. This fee is assessed every three months. Fees for this type of service can be waived if the account shows a certain level of activity throughout a six-month time frame. A minimum of four trades will satisfy this detail.

These are just two of the online investment options that you may choose from when you have decided to utilize the Internet for your next big financial move.

There is never a shortage of brokers for online forex day trading. Most of them will tell you they are shrewd specialists who can turn your principal capital to the millions of a brief time. In case you enter the trade with such a mindset, that you are setting yourself up for disappointment.

Any MetaTrader company who promises rapid results is the very first one you ought to ditch. Rewards from FX investing can be quick and also the likelihood of generating losses are always glaring. It is for that reason that you have be critical to decide on a brokerage firm wisely or else endure the fate of a lot of investors who've been left penniless following their brokers made losses and closed shop.

Beneath are some simple ideas to assist you in picking the very best mt4 service to assist your trade-

Commissions:

The active intraday forex trader pays more commissions to brokerage firms than typical traders. This is simply because there's perspective to create more in this line of the company than other people. Pay attention to the reality that commissions paid out to your mt5 brokerage slices off your overall earnings. When you are trading in stocks, you'll find two choices to think about: per share pricing and ticket pricing. In forex or futures trading, there is the spread and round turn cost and margin.

Customer service:

How might the brokerage firm treat their clients? You might be a green forex trader with small information on the way to commence out in this field. The brokerage firm ought to guide you 1 step at a time and ensure you understand as much as you can about what you might be finding yourself in to. No matter the size and reputation of the company, if they lack consumer service, you are better off elsewhere.

Trading systems:

The FX brokerage service ought to supply you with immediate access to your account at all occasions. Some notorious currency exchange brokers receive payments on order flow and could even trade against you. Online forex trading demands trading software program and platforms to function efficiently. The computer software offered should be user-friendly and present you with instant access to the most recent data regarding your account. Private software developers have come up with innovative trading platforms which will link up with the computer software. While they come at a value, they can make the trading method smoother between you as well as the brokerage firm.

Redundancy:

This can be a word that makes any individual inside the forex day trading market cringe. There have been companies that have come up swiftly and gone down at the same rate with investors' cash. The MetaTrader four company must supply assurances of what will occur supposedly things go rock bottom. They must also have distinct means of communication by which you can trace your account.

Chapter 10: Real Estate Investing

Real estate investing is an excellent career choice whether you want to flip or go long. It offers what most people aspire: wealth and flexibility. You can earn a lot of money in real estate which allows you to work whenever you want. It's not a 9 to 5 job that ties you up at the office. You can even work at home if you want and still find some quality time with the family. How to get started? Successful real estate investor, Jackie Lange, discusses the 3 step game plan to get started in real estate the right way.

1st Step - Put your Mind into It

The key to being a successful property investor is to put a lot of dedication into your work. Ask yourself this question - "Do I want to do this?" Having the right state of mind will let you easily overcome obstacles and allow you to persevere no matter what the situation is. While property investing is a lucrative business, it also comes with its share of risks and difficulties. Once you enter real estate, you must be prepared to face financing, management and acquisition decisions. You must also be prepared to become a landlord and deal with both good and bad tenants. Be ready to be your boss and perform marketing and management functions.

2nd Step - Take Real Estate Investor Training

Being knowledgeable about the real estate investing playing field is of utmost importance. You need to learn the important details and right strategies for the job. Real estate investor training is a worthwhile investment. There are online training websites available that can give you sufficient training for a year. Here's how to choose the best online training package.

*Choose a company that provides a vast library of training materials. Students learn best when they're given various forms of media to learn from. A training company that has a great compilation of books, audios, videos and articles gives you plenty of information to work on, which essentially translates to knowledge gained from different sources.

*Consider a company that offers coaching calls and private coaching forums. Teachers, fellow students and real estate investors can guide you into the right path. A coaching forum is important so you can see what kind of problems other investors have. You can also interact and ask questions yourself when it comes to deal structuring, choosing the best deal, etc.

*Choose a company whose teachers are, themselves, successful property investors. The best people to teach you are those who are currently engaged in real estate investing. They know the current trends and strategies. They also have the experience for the job. It's great to learn from other people's investing experiences so you can avoid problems and make the right choices.

3rd Step - Start Investing!

Your real estate investor training will have given you the knowledge and confidence to take your first investment. You may have also gained a network to consult with. You can start with easy investments like single family houses. Practice what you have learned and start investing!

Just like any other kind of business, real estate investing has its share of pitfalls and successes. Thus, you have to be cautious while pushing aside fear. Keep in mind that if other investors can do it, so can you. Successful real estate investing is not an impossible feat if you put your heart and soul into it. As Lao Tzu has said, "A journey of a thousand miles begins with a single step."

Chapter 11: Starting And Running A Small Business

Many people think that starting a small business is a very easy thing to do. Well, it is not. It cannot be further from the truth. But the fact remains that if you are very much prepared while you are still planning your business, then you will have higher chances of success. So whether you think of your business as your main source of income or just as a hobby, you should put much effort on it from the very beginning.

No matter how big or small is the business that you intend to start, if you lack the necessary preparations and planning then you will be having a hard time with it. The successful business people are always doing many preparations first before they go into any business or deals. This will help minimize their losses should their business ideas eventually turn out to be on the losing side.

Therefore, to better help you when you are starting a small business, here are some suggestions and tips to help you get started.

You should always look for a market whenever you have a business idea or product in mind that you would like to create a business around it. You can do market research first. It does not have to be a very thorough and extensive research, just collect enough data to help you prove that there is indeed a market for your product or service. Because if there is none, then you would just be wasting your time and money on getting your business started. An example is this: can you sell beef burgers in India? Look for a market and then create the product or service for it. If you need to get business loans Australia, then do it.

When you have found out that there is a lucrative market, then the next thing that you should be doing is preparing the best product for that market. Do not just go with any product just for the sake of having something to offer the public. You should always think of the quality of your product. Because if you choose incorrectly then the low quality of your product or service would be known all around the market, limiting your chances of getting new customers.

You should get a friend and bounce off your business ideas to them. This is a good way of checking if your business plans and ideas are sensible and if these are worth your time to pursue. If you can, find someone who has a background in marketing or running a business. After all, it pays to get advice from someone who has been there and was able to meet success.

Find out all what requirements you need to get started and whether you can complete all of them within a reasonable time. Depending on where you live or where you are planning to start your small business, there would be government requirements that you will first need to fulfill. And do not forget about the problem with red tape, which is just about the inefficiency of most agencies. Find a workaround for such hindrances.

These are some of the tips to help you when starting your own business in Australia today. Keep in mind that the key to starting a small business is preparation. When you are prepared then, you are ready for most eventualities that you may have to face when running your own business.

The American dream of owning a small business is still relevant today. Owning a small business can be a positive experience that can give you more freedom and unlimited income possibilities.

The fruits of becoming a successful entrepreneur cannot be achieved without following some simple steps to starting a small business.

Small Business Start Up Step #1:

Gather your thoughts to figure out what kind of business you would like to start. You should try to choose something you are passionate about. If you do not like what you do, chances are you will not make any money.

Small Business Start Up Step #2:

Do your due diligence on the amount of money you will need to get started and maintain your business for at least one year. Many businesses fall in their very first year in business due to lack of capital.

Small Business Start Up Step #3:

Organize your priorities to make sure you will have enough time to dedicate to your business. Remember, you won't make any money unless you produce. If you do not have enough time to dedicate to your business, then you make want to reconsider.

Small Business Start Up Step #4:

Decide whether your small business will be a partnership, Limited Liability Company (LLC) or a sole proprietorship. When selecting your business entity, you should choose wisely because each entity has its characteristics. For more detailed information, you can visit your local government center.

Small Business Start Up Step #5:

Choose a business name. This part is very important because if you can choose a name that is catchy, people will find it easier to remember when searching for your business. Your legal company name and your DBA (doing business as) can be different.

Small Business Start Up Step #6:

Decide where on a location. Location can play a huge part on whether your sales thrive or not. If you are planning on starting an internet based business, then you would need to check on how competitive your niche market is before you build your website.

Small Business Start Up Step #7:

Register your business properly by getting your EIN (Employer Identification Number) and Articles of Organization submitted to the Secretary Of State.

Small Business Start Up Step #8:

Put together a solid business plan. A good plan should include a marketing strategy that will give you a chance to succeed. Your marketing strategy should include information on your competitors and how you plan on offering something different.

Small Business Start Up Step #9:

Make sure you have a great strategy on how you are going to keep track of the books. It is not a good practice to figure this part out as you go along. The more you know where your money is going, the easier and faster you can make adjustments.

Small Business Start Up Step #10:

The final step to starting a small business is the most important. You must be certain that all applicable licenses, license fees, rules of the county, rules of the state, government taxes and all other regulations are met. There is nothing worse than building your customer base only to get shut down.

The steps to starting a small business are not as difficult as many people may think, but they are mandatory. The joy and sense of accomplishment you will get from running your own business successfully cannot be expressed in words, doing your due diligence will help your transition go a lot smoother.

Chapter 12: Tips For Success

Investing can be profitable if you find the right thing to invest in. This statement has been tested, and nowadays many people make enough money to make a living through different types of investment. However, you should not get excited as investments can also be quite dangerous if you do not know what you are doing in the first place. There are risks involved, and such risks are not associated with any other form of money handling. This is why a lot of stock investment advertisements say that there are certain market risks, and every single document related to a certain investment should be inspected thoroughly.

If you study the general trend, you will easily notice that most of the stock market players are looking for a way to make a profit in the short term. There are very few who have long term plans. This is why many people fail in the first few attempts and then give up on investing right away. In case some of them get lucky and do make some profit from the beginning, they start making bigger mistakes later on which ultimately leads to their downfall in due time.

Like with anything else, there are certain rules that apply to the stock markets and grasping them all takes quite a lot of time for a beginner. There are specific calculations and logics that need to be used properly to predict an outcome correctly. In the case of sudden drastic changes where no rules apply and in that case nothing can be done to avoid a disaster.

As a beginner, you should always keep in mind that long-term goals are a lot better than short-term ones. In case you have decided that it is time for you to start investing in the stock market do not just try to make money fast and then leave. Instead, think about sticking to this way of making money for a longer period and make some long-term plans for success. The reason why the bigger players always manage to make significant profits is that they never hurry things up and let an investment do everything it can before they abandon it.

If you want to get a grasp of the most important factors that govern the stock market you should perform thorough research first. You should never ignore the facts you uncover through your research. Use every little piece of information available for you because it might turn out to be helpful. Not everyone can handle losing money. This is so important because for beginners the money to cover losses comes from their savings which are earned through hard work. Not everyone can take such a blow. This is why beginners need to take certain precautions and only invest in sectors that are more promising and understand. In case you need it information etc, talk to a professional to get explanations for all the terminology and the shortcomings of making an investment in the stock market.

The most commonly heard and repeated rule of investing is always "buy low and sell high." It seems if that's all there was to it, everyone would be able to make a fortune in the stock market! Even though it is the most widely used piece of investment advice, the biggest mistake that investors make is to buy high and sell low - because just knowing the basics isn't enough - you need to be able to make sense of it, too.

Here are three tips for beginning investors:

1) Don't Try to Trade (Buy/Sell) Too Frequently

In other words, choose long term investment options to give your stocks the chance to increase value. Even the best stocks have ups and downs regarding their value, and even the most successful investors can't consistently predict whether or not a specific stock will increase or decrease in value day after day. When you look at stocks over a longer period though, most of them will increase in value, making sure you follow the cardinal investment rule of buying low and selling high. When you try to time the market and listen to everyone's stock tips about a certain stock rising or falling, most of the time you will be buying high and selling low.

Another benefit of choosing to invest over the long term are the tax benefits. If you buy a security and keep it for less than a year before you sell it, you will pay regular income tax rates on any of the capital gains it may have made. If you hold on to security for more than a year, then you will only pay 15% tax on the capital gains.

2) Don't Put All of Your Eggs in One Basket

We've all heard the amazing success stories of people who have invested all of their money into one stock and woke up the next day to double or triple their investment - but more often than not, when you don't diversify, you'll wake up to find your entire investment gone. Diversification is key to reducing your risk when investing. When you put all of your money on the hope of a single company, you could discover that a company is doing well today then files bankruptcy tomorrow, and you've lost your investment. Diversifying and spreading your money across stocks from some different companies and industries reduces your risk - all of the companies would have to fail for you to lose all of your investment.

Diversification can also mean spreading your investment out across more than just stocks. Most people keep a portfolio of stocks, bonds, IRAs, money market deposit accounts and high-interest savings accounts to reduce their risk further and balance their portfolios.

3) Keep an Emergency Fund and Don't Invest More Than You Can Afford

Another common mistake new investors make is to try investing too much of their money - and then finding out they don't have access to cash if an emergency happens. Before you begin investing in stocks or other methods that are not easy to pull your money from when needed. It's wise to establish an emergency account in high-interest savings or another form of liquid account. This will give you access to cash in the event of an emergency. Once you have an emergency fund established, you can then focus on determining how much money you can afford to investment.

The information in this article is certainly not groundbreaking, but for new investors, these tips can make the difference between earning a return and losing your investment.

Chapter 13: Mistakes To Avoid

Real estate investment has become a viable option for many investors as huge profits are expected from it. This is the main reason behind many people investing in property. It is worth considering that big money is involved in the investment, and it might be the biggest investment you probably make in your lifetime. Therefore, wise decision-making at every step of property purchase is necessary for securing a successful deal. Unfortunately, many people make common mistakes while investing in real estate, avoiding which is necessary to expect profitable returns.

Many people follow a myth that if real estate experiences a change in prices, the same is likely not to happen in an upcoming period. Making an investment with this misconception can sometimes result in a big loss. This false belief restricts the investors from keeping themselves updated with current market trends, stopping them from making an investment when the prices are low. Change in property price cannot be underestimated, especially when it can sometimes change more than once in a day. Hence, it is viable not to avoid market conditions when investing in real estate.

It is vital to consider the present worth of the real estate rather than focusing on its future value. Many people commit this mistake of making the investment by assuming the future value of the property. For a fact property prices experience huge fluctuations, adopting this strategy is not an efficient way of making an investment. It is hard to predict what a real estate value could be in future. So, it is wise to emphasize on present value rather than future value.

Some people often adopt the same strategy throughout investing in property. Although it can be beneficial during the initial phase of the investment, sticking to it when encountering problems might not bring an effective solution to any hitch. There is always need to adopt new strategies or modify current ones to cope up with the changing market trends and to deal effectively with problems that might appear anytime during the process of investment. Avoiding the mistake of sticking to same strategies can bring positive returns.

Paying for the purchase of real estate does not bring an end to the investment. Additional costs, such as maintenance costs and repair costs also come along, which are often neglected by many investors. Ignoring this aspect while investing in property can sometimes result in negative consequences as these costs are enough to take out a big chunk from your pocket. Also, it might get difficult for the investors to afford these costs later, deterring them from experiencing the true benefits of investing in real estate. An ideal way of making an investment is by considering the repair and maintenance costs along with actual investment cost.

Real estate investment is not something that can be taken lightly and requires series of wise decisions at every step. For first time investors, professional help can be of utter benefit as it can successfully help avoid common property investment mistakes.

Chapter 14: Keep Up With Your Progress

When it comes to investing goals, setting them is the easy part; it's reaching them that can get a bit complicated and challenging. What looks feasible on paper can seem insurmountable in real life when obstacles present themselves. Overcoming these obstacles and keeping your goals at the forefront of every investing decision that you make is key to moving up the real estate investing ladder and building residual income.

The number one thing that can distract you from your goals is a discouragement. In the world of investments, particularly those involving real estate, nothing goes quite as planned, and there is always some element of risk. A miscalculation of costs or an unplanned emergency repair can set you back thousands of dollars. If you allow setbacks like these to discourage you, your project will likely hum along on a sour note making it even harder for you to recoup your original losses. If you remain optimistic though, you will be able to bounce back from setbacks and stay on track ultimately reaching your goal.

In addition to remaining optimistic, there are several things that you can do to ensure that you meet all of your real estate investing goals.

Here are a few tips that you can try for yourself: Break large, long-term goals up into smaller, short-term goals. Short term goals don't seem as impossible or as overwhelming as long term goals and are easier to attain. Meeting short-term goals also motivates you to keep moving forward as you can track your progress with each milestone met.

Display a list of your goals in a spot that you will see them and be reminded of them often. In a hectic world, it's easy to lose sight of plans that you have made, but by constantly reminding yourself of the goals that you have set, you will be able to keep them at the foundation of all of your decisions.

Re-evaluate your goals often. The real estate investing market changes constantly and you have to be ready to change with it. A stale goal strategy will only put you further and further behind your competition. Be ready to change with the market and adjust your goals accordingly.

Consistently meeting goals requires consistency on your part. Begin each day by asking yourself what can be done that day to help you reach your goals. And don't be discouraged by the progress that doesn't seem to be moving along as well as you would like it to. Any victory, no matter how small, brings you one step closer to realizing your ultimate investing goals.

Chapter 15: Keep Up With The News

Trading securities in the stock exchange could be a dodgy and profit-making undertaking. In this contemporary contraction in the economy, it's also an enticing idea. The lures of wealth and the status of being a market operator are occasionally impossible to resist. If only it were simply a matter of signing on with a broker and getting started selling and purchasing. The fact is if it were that straightforward everybody would be doing it.

When somebody first gets started, it is extremely possible he's going to have 1 or 2 fortunate trades and make a little money. This only goes to fuel the fire, as it were and has the capability for disaster. False confidence early on can cause bad habits, ignorant guesstimates and eventually the poor house. As losses increase due to trying to earn income back, a snowballing effect starts to happen. Despair sets in, the mind becomes clouded and confused as blind selling and purchasing activity increases. Stocks are being chased and always appear to be just behind the curve. You lose more till there's no more to lose. When you eventually stop to take the assessment, it's too late. Everything is lost.

That naturally is a very bad picture but occurs a lot. The exchange isn't a place to get wealthy fast or to run to when in between roles. It takes years of education, random test and counsel from the ones that have been there.

Numerous books have penned by pro-market operators and not so pro too. Select sensibly whom will teach and direct you. Be dubious of those making additional money selling books and counsel than those making it the markets. Many people understand what to do and will sell that data without having successfully implemented it themselves. It's straightforward study and discovers what to do; the challenge is doing it and doing at the right point with the correct quantities.

At last, one will need to find or choose a coach. An instructor is the one which will show the way. Your coach will teach you and steer you thru the fine details of the markets. This is maybe the most significant call that may be made in your career. The organization or person that trains you may show the way as they know it but following your ultimate success is decided by you. What rules you select to make and follow, the form of trading you would like to follow and how closely you follow those rules.

It'll cost some money, and there'll be more than one that are attempted before a good fit is found. Beware any that promise simple wealth or consistent grotesque returns. There's nothing simple about making profits in the stock exchange. Ensure you have to research any potential concepts totally through forums, internet sites, search sites and blogs. There are lots of extremely good folks out there and a lot that need to take your hard-earned money with no recognized value.

It's not to say that trading stocks, forex or futures isn't a profitable business, it actually can be, but at the end, it's all down to you. It takes tough work, masses of hours and the correct coaching. Profiting constantly needs time and practice. You can do it if you do it properly.

Conclusion

Sophisticated endowment funds and high-net-worth families have long relied on a simple strategy for investing their core wealth, a strategy that may surprise you. This strategy does not involve high-speed stock trading, esoteric derivatives, or connections to pre-IPO, start-up, and ventures. Rather these investors build a simple, well-diversified portfolio and follow a disciplined, re-balancing approach that keeps investment costs down and avoids volatility. In this article, we describe this investment process and how you can implement it in your retirement portfolio.

1. Seek Return but Mitigate Risk - As an investor, you should seek the highest rate of return possible for the risk you are willing to endure. This sounds obvious but remarkably few investors even consider a long-term strategy based on their risk tolerance, and even fewer then stick with the strategy when markets tumble.

Many investors think about their portfolio regarding stocks and bonds. Allocating additional resources to bonds is one approach to reducing risk, but the decrease in return is costlier than necessary. Shifting wealth from risky assets to less risky assets is done at the peril of portfolio growth. Constructing a portfolio from a more diverse set of assets can reduce risk without reducing return, but to take advantage of this, you must be able to measure the similarity of assets and quantify the benefits of diversification.

2. Diversify wisely - All you require for your diversified, retirement portfolio is roughly 11 low-cost index funds. You can simply ignore the thousands and thousands of other ETFs, stocks, bonds and other investments being peddled to you by brokers and advisers.

The trick is to make sure that the 11 asset classes are properly correlated. Merely spreading your wealth across different asset classes is a dangerous approach to diversification. The risk reduction benefit that one gets from diversification depends on how the returns of two assets are related - their correlation. While combining asset classes with low correlation into a portfolio can significantly reduce risk, combining asset classes with high correlation may not provide much risk reduction. To meaningfully benefit from diversification, it is necessary to measure correlation and allocate assets accordingly.

3. Invest efficiently - Nobel Laureate Harry Markowitz in his pioneering work on portfolio theory developed a framework for building efficient portfolios- portfolios that attain the lowest risk for the return obtained. Essentially these portfolios trace a curve

known as the "efficient frontier." Every investor's goal is to position their portfolio as close to this curve as possible. Portfolios below the curve take on more risk than is necessary to obtain the same expected return. As an investor, you should always seek efficiency. Otherwise, you are in essence giving away something (more risk exposure) in exchange for nothing (higher investment returns).

Prudent, long-term investors are not guided by beliefs or predictions about the direction of markets or asset class returns. Like the academics, we don't believe that basing investment decisions on predictions of economic direction is a sound approach. It leads to more risk, higher costs and less return for the investor. Markets are too often random and unpredictable. Wharton economist Jeremy Siegel analyzed the stock market's 120 biggest up and biggest down days over the last 200 years and for only 25% of those days could he come up with any explanation at all.

4. Rebalance Intelligently - "Buy and Hold" is a great philosophy in general. But if you let your portfolio roam free for too long, your long-term strategy will likely be thrown off - either becoming too weighted to risky assets or too conservative. The solution is regular rebalancing. There is a tradeoff between

rebalancing frequently, which keeps your portfolio near an optimal allocation, and paying fees and taxes generated from trading. The tax structure of your account and the trading costs associated with your fund or ETF selections should dictate how frequently you trade. For example, at Portfolio Research we offer six strategies, each with several rebalancing policies that address different tax and fee situations.

Our research, as well as other published results, shows that using rebalancing thresholds (rebalancing when your portfolio has drifted above or below the desired allocation) is superior to calendar rebalancing.

5. Maintain an Optimal Allocation - Maintaining the optimal portfolio is not necessarily easy, but increasingly investors can access online portfolio models that they can use as guides to building their portfolios without spending money on brokers and advisers. For example, each month, using a suitable return history, Portfolio Research estimates the correlation among all asset classes, the risk (volatility) of each asset class, and the expected returns. These estimations allow us to construct an efficient frontier similar to what is described above. Based on this information we recommend the optimal percentage of a portfolio to invest in each asset class that depends on a selected risk tolerance. As the risk and

the return relationships among asset classes change, so do our recommended allocations through time.

6. Minimize Fees and Taxes - Nothing reduces investment returns like fees. Index funds and ETFs that track a market index have a more attractive fee structures than actively managed funds. Interestingly, many investors flock to actively managed funds, for the perceived additional returns. It is a simple tautology that the collection of actively managed funds must underperform their index after fees. Individual investors using our asset allocation model are free to invest in the recommended asset classes using a managed or passive approach. However, our recommended fund list is comprised of passive funds and ETFs that offer attractive rates.

Conclusion - An efficient approach to investing requires strategy and tactics. Implementation of an efficient approach requires analytics-volatilities and correlations must be assessed to determine diversification opportunities and optimization procedures are required to identify the efficient frontier. Similarly, analytics are required to understand risk and tax implications associated with rebalancing policies.

What results can one expect from an analytical investment approach like ours? Our asset allocation strategies are designed to obtain sustainable advantages that come from maintaining efficiency, reducing fees and volatility, and managing trading costs and taxes. Over time, these advantages compound into meaningful outperformance-. Over 30 years the difference in wealth from a small return difference can be extremely large. Investors will benefit enormously in retirement by spending a little time now creating an efficient portfolio.

Please if you enjoyed this book and feel it gave you lots of value then I would greatly appreciate it if you gave an honest review of it. Those honest words would be more than just words to me but feedback for my next book!

Also, please check out my other books!

Thanks for reading my book.

www.ingramcontent.com/pod-product-compliance
Lightning Source LLC
Chambersburg PA
CBHW070329190526
45169CB00005B/1808